Get Ready For Secondary School Mathematics

Andrew Baines

Contents

Introduction

About Secondary School Mathematics

This book is a step-by-step guide to learning and practising the important things you will need to know in Secondary Maths lessons. It can be used as a workbook because every section deals with a particular topic and has its own practice exercises. Or you can use it as a revision book and just remind yourself of the particular things you need to know. You can also use it alongside Bond Assessment Papers in Maths (there are six books for primary children, from age 6 to age 11) which provide sets of graded papers for development and extensive practice of Maths skills.

The National Strategy for Key Stage 3 has made the way Maths is taught in Year 7 more similar to the way it is taught in Primary schools, but there are still important differences. This book prepares you for this change and ensures you will hit the ground running when you start your new school.

How to use this book

The book is divided into sections covering the key topics from The Framework for Teaching Mathematics: Years 7, 8 and 9. Many of these are based on objectives from the Year 6 and 7 Framework. Every section introduces or develops ideas based on what you already know. There are practice exercises after each topic has been explained.

For every chapter, first of all read the text on the left-hand page. This tells you (or reminds you) of how to answer a certain type of question. Then practice your skills using the exercises on the right.

There are four mixed-content tests to assess how you are doing on pages 52–59. The answers are provided in a pull-out section on pages A1–A4.

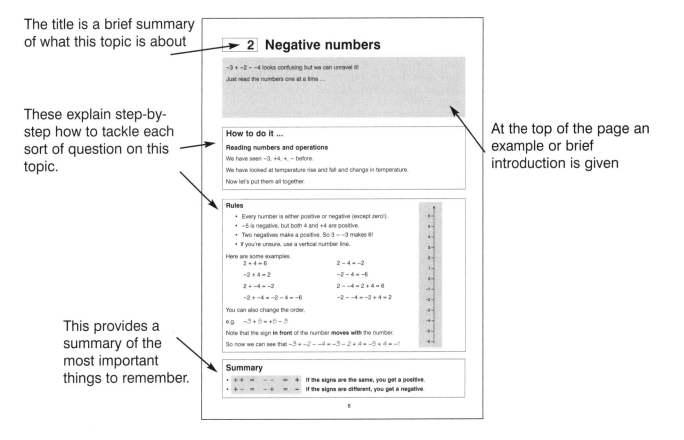

The title is a brief summary of what this topic is about

These explain step-by-step how to tackle each sort of question on this topic.

This provides a summary of the most important things to remember.

At the top of the page an example or brief introduction is given

1 Comparing measurements

473 ml   0.7596 litres

Do you know which is greater?

Well, if you don't, you soon will do!

How to do it ...

Comparing and ordering decimals

You have seen how to order decimals by looking at the place value of the digits, reading from left to right.

→

	tens	units	.	tenths	hundredths	thousandths
12.043 is	1	2	.	0	4	3
13.72 is	1	3	.	7	2	

The tens numbers are equal. Comparing the units numbers, 3 is greater than 2. Therefore, 13.72 is bigger than 12.043.

We can write this as: *13.72 > 12.043*   or   *12.043 < 13.72*

Converting between units of measure

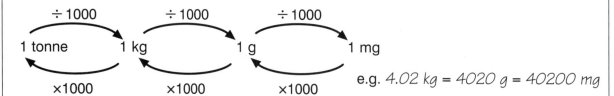

e.g. *4.02 kg = 4020 g = 40200 mg*

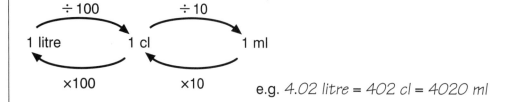

e.g. *4.02 litre = 402 cl = 4020 ml*

Now practise!

Which number is bigger?

1   45.3   or   45.08   _45.3_

2   3.045   or   3.054   _3.054_

3   1204.2   or   123.45   _1204.2_

3

Use the correct inequality sign (< or >) to show which number is bigger.

4   0.325   _<_   0.345

5   3.18   _>_   3.169

6   11.23   _>_   11.03

3

Place the following numbers on the correct sides of the inequality signs.

7   45.6   45.2   _45.2_   <   _45.6_

8   0.821   0.812   _0.821_   >   _0.812_

9   4.6   4.65   4.4   _4.4_   <   _4.6_   <   _4.65_

3

Convert these measurements into the following units.

10   3.24 kg   =   _3240_ g

11   0.506 litre   =   _50.6_ cl   =   _506_ ml

12   234.06 m   =   _23406_ cm   =   _234060_ mm

3

13/8/07

Converting between units of measure

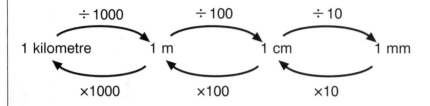

$\div 1000$ $\div 100$ $\div 10$

1 kilometre   1 m   1 cm   1 mm

$\times 1000$ $\times 100$ $\times 10$

e.g.   *4.02 km = 4020 m = 402000 cm*

Comparing measurements

To compare 473 ml and 0.7596 litre we must first compare both using the same units.

Use the **smaller unit** to compare the amounts.

What we are comparing:	*473 ml*	and	*0.7596 l*
Converted to ml:	*473 ml*	and	*759.6 ml*
So:	*473 ml*	<	*759.6 ml*
Which means that:	*473 ml*	<	*0.7596 l*

Note: Always write the answer using the original information.

Summary

- Look at the place value of the digits, reading from left to right. ⟶
- We can say that 5 > 4 or 4 < 5.
- To compare measurements, we must first convert the larger unit to the smaller units.
- It's easiest to use the smallest units.
- Always write the answer using the original information.

1 Exercises

Now practise!

Order these measurements, starting with the smallest.

13   6 kg   600 g   *600g*   *6 kg*

14   1.2 m   46 cm   0.95 m   *46 cm*   *0.95 m*   *1.2 m*

15   1.24 cl   1.01 litre   12.3 ml   *12.3 ml*   *1.24 cl*   *1.01 litre*
         124   *1010*   *12.3*

3

Use the correct inequality sign to show which measurement is larger.

16   7.54 cm   *>*   34.02 mm

17   301 ml   *<*   0.404 litre

18   0.3509 kg   *>*   35019 mg

3

2 Negative numbers

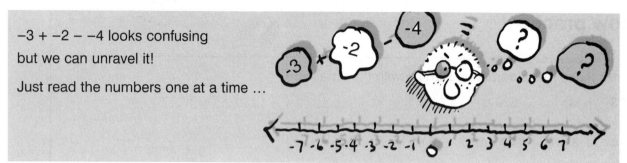

-3 + -2 - -4 looks confusing but we can unravel it!

Just read the numbers one at a time ...

How to do it ...

Reading numbers and operations

You have seen -3, +4, +, - before.

You have looked at temperature rise and fall and changes in temperature.

Now let's put them all together.

Rules

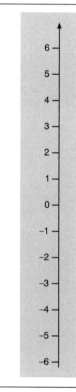

- Every number is either positive or negative (except zero!).
- -5 is negative, but both 4 and +4 are positive.
- Two negatives make a positive. So 3 - -3 makes 6!
- If you're unsure, use a vertical number line.

Here are some examples.

$$2 + 4 = 6 \qquad\qquad 2 - 4 = -2$$
$$-2 + 4 = 2 \qquad\qquad -2 - 4 = -6$$
$$2 + -4 = -2 \qquad\qquad 2 - -4 = 2 + 4 = 6$$
$$-2 + -4 = -2 - 4 = -6 \qquad -2 - -4 = -2 + 4 = 2$$

You can also change the order,

e.g. $-3 + 5 = +5 - 3$

Note that the sign **in front** of the number **moves with** the number.

So now we can see that $-3 + -2 - -4 = -3 - 2 + 4 = -5 + 4 = -1$

Summary

- $+ + = - - = +$ **If the signs are the same, you get a positive.**
- $+ - = - + = -$ **If the signs are different, you get a negative.**

2 Exercises

Now practise!

Simplify the following.

1	+ +4	2	+ −12	3	− −35

1. 4

2. −12

3. 35

3

Now simplify these.

4	2 + −8	5	−12 + −7	6	−7 − 13 + −3

3

Find the answers to these.

7	2 + −7 =	8	−6 + −3 =	9	3 − 5 − +5 =

3

Now simplify these.

10	72 − −8	11	−132 − +46	12	−237 − 13 + −37

3

Find the answers to these.

13	92 − −8 =	14	−1082 − +46 =	15	−457 − 13 + −1 =

3

3 HCF and LCM 13/8/07

We have heard of JCB, BFG and OTT but what on earth are HCF and LCM?

How to do it ...

Prime factors

The **prime factors** of a number are all the prime numbers that will divide into it.

So the **prime factors** of 12 are 2 and 3.

There are groups of numbers that have the same prime factors, e.g. 6 and 12.

We can see how they differ by writing each number as a **product of prime factors**.

e.g. $12 = 2 \times 2 \times 3$ and $6 = 2 \times 3$

HCF

The **HCF** or **highest common factor** of two or more numbers is the largest number that will divide into them leaving a whole number answer.

There are two methods of finding the HCF. To find the HCF of 12 and 18 you can use:

Method 1: Write the factors of both in order

    The factors of 12 are 1, 2, 3, 4, **6** and 12
    The factors of 18 are 1, 2, 3, **6**, 9 and 18
    The common factors of 12 and 18 are 1, 2, 3 and **6**

The **HCF** of 12 and 18 is **6**

Method 2: Write each number as a product of prime factors and multiply the ones that appear in both

    $12 = 2 \times 6 = \mathbf{2} \times 2 \times \mathbf{3}$
    $18 = 2 \times 9 = \mathbf{2} \times \mathbf{3} \times 3$

HCF of 12 and 18 = **2 × 3 = 6**

> What appears in both?

3 Exercises

Now practise!

What are the prime factors of the following numbers?

1   15   3, 5

2   21   7, 3

3   20   5, 2   **3**

Write the following numbers as a product of prime factors.

4 $14 =$ 7×2

5 $22 =$ 2×11

6 $24 =$ **3**

Find the HCF of the following pairs of numbers.

7   14 and 21   7

8   22 and 44   11

9   36 and 48   6

10   24 and 32   8

11   45 and 81   9

12   26 and 65   13   **6**

3 HCF and LCM continued

How to do it ...

LCM

The LCM or **lowest common multiple** of two or more numbers is the smallest number they will all divide into.

There are two methods of finding the LCM, similar to the methods of finding the HCF.

Method 1

> Multiples of 12 are *12, 24, **36**, 48, 56, 60, ...*
> Multiples of 18 are *18, **36**, 54, 72, ...*

The **LCM** of 12 and 18 is **36**

Method 2

> $12 = 2 \times 6 = \mathbf{2 \times 2 \times 3}$
>
> $18 = 2 \times 9 = \mathbf{2 \times 3 \times 3}$

LCM of 12 and 18 $= \mathbf{2 \times 2 \times 3 \times 3 = 36}$

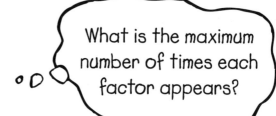

What is the maximum number of times each factor appears?

e.g. *For the LCM of 300 and 70:*

> $300 = 2 \times 2 \times 3 \times 5 \times 5$
>
> $70 = 2 \qquad \times 5 \qquad \times 7$

LCM $= 2 \times 2 \times 3 \times 5 \times 5 \times 7 = 2100$

Summary

- **Prime factors** of 12 are 2 and 3
- **Product of prime factors**: e.g. $12 = 2 \times 2 \times 3$
- The **HCF** of 12 and 18 is **6**
- The **LCM** of 12 and 18 is **36**

3 Exercises

Now practise!

Find the LCM of the following pair of numbers.

13   4 and 6   _12_

14   6 and 9   _18_

15   16 and 12   _48_

16   5 and 6   _30_

17   8 and 12   _24_

18   20 and 15   _60_

19   12 and 18   _36_

20   16 and 24   _48_

21   66 and 165   _330_

9

4 Square roots

No, this is not some kind of special tree with square roots!

This is just the inverse, or opposite, of square numbers!

How to do it ...

Square numbers

If you multiply any whole number by itself you get a square number.

Let's take the number 5. $5 \times 5 = 5^2 = 25$.   So **25 is a square number**.

The next square number after 25 is found by starting with the next number after the number we squared to get 25.

That's the number 6. $6 \times 6 = 6^2 = 36$.   So **36 is the next square number**.

Square roots

The number which multiplied by itself makes a square number is the square root of that square number.

So the **square root of 25 is 5**.   This is written as $\sqrt{25} = 5$

And the **square root of 36 is 6**.   This is written as $\sqrt{36} = 6$

We can multiply square roots together to find bigger square roots.

e.g. $4^2 = 16$ and $10^2 = 100$ So $4^2 \times 10^2 = 16 \times 100 = 1600$

And if we know this, we can do $\sqrt{1600}$!!!!

$\sqrt{1600} = \sqrt{16} \times \sqrt{100} = 4 \times 10 = 40$!!!!!!

Summary

- $7 \times 7 = 7^2 = 49$ So **49 is a square number**.

- **The square root of 9 is 3**.   This is written as $\sqrt{9} = 3$

- $5^2 = 25$ and $10^2 = 100$ So $5^2 \times 10^2 = 25 \times 100 = 2500$

- $\sqrt{2500} = \sqrt{25} \times \sqrt{100} = 5 \times 10 = 50$

4 Exercises

Now practise!

Multiply the following numbers by themselves to make a square number.

1 2

4

2 3

9

3 8

64

3

$2 \times 2 = 2^2$. Write these in the same way.

4 $6 \times 6 =$

6^2

5 $11 \times 11 =$

11^2

6 $14 \times 14 =$

14^2

3

Find the following.

7 $2^2 =$

4

8 $9^2 =$

81

9 $12^2 =$

144

3

Find the square root of the following.

10 16

4

11 9

3

12 100

10

3

Find the following.

13 $\sqrt{64} =$

8

14 $\sqrt{4} =$

2

15 $\sqrt{121} =$

11

3

Now try these!

16 $\sqrt{400} =$

20

17 $\sqrt{900} =$

30

18 $\sqrt{225} =$

15

3

5 Fractions to decimals

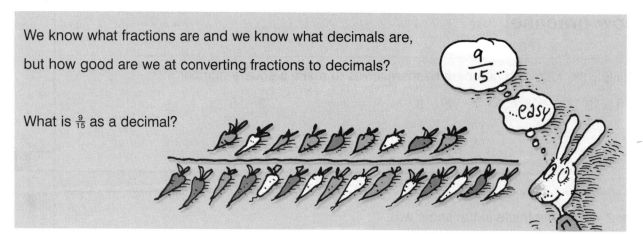

We know what fractions are and we know what decimals are, but how good are we at converting fractions to decimals?

What is $\frac{9}{15}$ as a decimal?

How to do it ...

Equivalent fractions

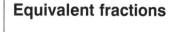

$$\frac{1}{2} \quad = \quad \frac{10}{20} \quad = \quad \frac{50}{100}$$

$$\times 10 \qquad \times 5$$

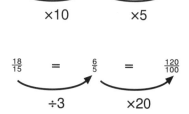

$$\frac{18}{15} \quad = \quad \frac{6}{5} \quad = \quad \frac{120}{100}$$

$$\div 3 \qquad \times 20$$

Multiply both the numerator and the denominator until the denominator is 100.

Converting fractions to decimals

First, write the fraction as an equivalent fraction out of 100.

e.g. $\frac{2}{5} = \frac{20}{50} = \frac{40}{100}$

Second, write the numerator as a decimal to 2 decimal places.

e.g. $\frac{40}{100} = 0.40$ $\frac{3}{100} = 0.03$ $\frac{124}{100} = 1.24$

Summary

- Multiply or divide both the numerator and denominator of a fraction until the denominator is 100.
- Write the fraction as an equivalent fraction out of 100.
- Write the numerator as a decimal to 2 decimal places.

☐ 5 Exercises

Now practise!

Convert these fractions to hundredths.

1. $\frac{12}{50}$ $\frac{24}{100}$

2. $\frac{3}{10}$ $\frac{30}{100}$

3. $\frac{4}{5}$ $\frac{80}{100}$

3

Convert these vulgar (top-heavy) fractions to hundredths.

4. $\frac{423}{10}$ $\frac{4230}{100}$

5. $\frac{12}{5}$ $\frac{240}{100}$

6. $\frac{56}{40}$ $\frac{140}{100}$

3

Convert these fractions to decimals.

7. $\frac{57}{100}$ 0.57

8. $\frac{5}{100}$ 0.05

9. $\frac{123}{100}$ 1.23

10. $\frac{7}{10}$ 0.70

11. $\frac{3}{4}$ 0.75

12. $\frac{14}{20}$ 0.70

13. $\frac{9}{30}$ 0.30

14. $\frac{42}{20}$ 2.10

15. $5\frac{3}{12}$ 5.25

9

6 Ratio

You see it on hill signs.

You see it in newspapers and magazines.

You see it at the races.

Is it strange? Is it foreign?
But can we understand it? YES!!!!!

How to do it ...

Ratio

You have seen ratios before in Year 6 but without the symbol :

e.g.   *1 free child ticket "with every" 2 adult tickets.*

This is the same as   *1 : 2*

2 free child tickets "with every" 1 adult ticket.

This is the same as   *2 : 1*

So 4 : 7 means **4 of the first thing** "for every" **7 of the second thing**.

Equivalent ratios

If you get

1 free child ticket "with every" 2 adult tickets.

Then with

8 adult tickets (4 x 2) you would get 4 free child tickets (4 x 1).

1 : 2 is the same as 4 : 8, so we can write *1 : 2 = 4 : 8*

Which means that 1 : 2 = 2 : 4 = 4 : 8 = 10 : 20 and so on.

The **simplest form** of this ratio is 1 : 2.

6 Exercises

Now practise!

Rewrite the following statements using the ratio symbol :

1 1 jug of water for every 3 people. _____

2 Pack 5 pairs of socks for every 2 pairs of jeans. _____

3 3 red beads for every 13 blue beads. _____

Sometimes we don't see the words "for every". The word "to" is often used, but we still do the same thing!! e.g. 4 : 7 means 4 of the first thing "to" 7 of the second thing.

4 There is a 5 to 2 chance of winning. _____

5 We will share the sweets like this. 3 for me 2 for you,

3 for me 2 for you… _____ **5**

Each of the following sets of ratios has a mistake. Put a line through the odd one out.

6 1 : 2   3 : 6   10 : 30

7 3 : 4   30 : 40   15 : 500

8 3 : 1   9 : 2   15 : 5   **3**

Fill in the missing number.

9 4 : 6   8 : 12

         × _____

10 1 : 4   3 : _____

         ×3   **2**

6 Ratio continued

Rules with ratio

Ratios stay the same if you multiply both sides **or** divide both sides by the same number.

Ratios do NOT stay the same if you add both sides or subtract both sides by the same number.

$3:4$ means the same as $15:20$ (both sides multiplied by 5)

$20:10$ means the same as $2:1$ (both sides divided by 10)

Using ratio to share something

If you share £30 in the ratio $1:1$ you get £15 : £15.

But if you share £30 in the ratio $2:1$ you get £20 : £10

Let's see how this works.

For every £2 the first person gets then the second person gets £1.

So the total going out each time is £2 + £1 = £3

As there are ten lots of £3 in £30 we multiply each side of the ratio by 10 to find our answer, £20 : £10.

Summary

$4:10 = 8:20 = 2:5 = 200:500$

Simplest form is $2:5$

To share £70 in the ratio $2:3$ we work like this:

$2 + 3 = 5$

$70 \div 5 = 14$

Multiply both sides by £14 and we get £28 : £42

6 Exercises

Now practise!

Fill in the missing number.

11   2 : 3   ____ : 15

           ×5

12   3 : ____   6 : 10

           ×2

13   4 : 6   2 : ____

           ÷2

14   14 : 7   2 : 1

           ÷ ____

4

Share the following amounts of money in the given ratio.

15   £20 in the ratio 12 : 8   _____

16   £32 in the ratio 5 : 11   _____

17   £45 in the ratio 2 : 3   _____

3

7 Order of operations

BODMAS, BIDMAS

What do they mean?

What is the difference?

Why do we need them?

How to do it ...

Brackets

This whole topic is basically a set of strict rules which we use throughout the world. And if you don't use them then nobody knows what you mean.

The 1st rule is always work out the information in the brackets first. Easy!

e.g. $9 - (5 - 2)$ means $9 - 3 = 6$ and $3(4 - 2)$ means $3 \times 2 = 6$

Order, index or power

(This means 5^2, 12^3, $\sqrt{16}$ and so on)

Work these out when you have worked out all the information in the brackets.

$3 + 5^2$ means $3 + 25$

5^2 means the same as 5 order 2, **or** 5 to the power of 2, **or** 5 index 2

You have to follow BODMAS (or BIDMAS) inside brackets as well.

e.g. $20 - (3^2 + 2)$ means the same as $20 - (9 + 2)$ which means the same as $20 - 11$

Divide and Multiply before Add and Subtract

So $4 + 6 \times 5 = 4 + 30 = 34$

$17 - 12 \div 3 + 2 = 17 - 4 + 2 = 15$

Summary

- First do   **B**rackets
- Then powers **O**rder or **I**ndices
- Next do   **D**ivide and **M**ultiply
- And then do **A**dd and **S**ubtract

BODMAS (or BIDMAS)

22

7 Exercises

Now practise!

Here is a long list to try. They do get harder. Just remember to follow the rules!

1 $5 - (12 - 3) =$

2 $23 - (12 + 3) =$

3 $8 - (12 \div 3) =$

`3`

4 $4(8 + 2) =$

5 $2(5 + 1) =$

6 $6 - (12 - 3) + (9 \div 3) =$

`3`

7 $5 + 3^2 =$

8 $7^2 + \sqrt{16} =$

9 $15 - (5^2 - 10) =$

`3`

10 $4 + 2 \times 3 =$

11 $12 + 8 \div 4 =$

12 $5 + 2 \times 3 - 1 =$

`3`

13 $2 \times 3^2 =$

14 $4(2^2 - 1) =$

15 $5^2 + 2 (21 \div 3) - 1 =$

`3`

8 Term, expression and equation

Term, **expression** and **equation** are the words we use when talking about algebra!

When we understand these we will find algebra easy! Let's Just DO IT!!!!!!

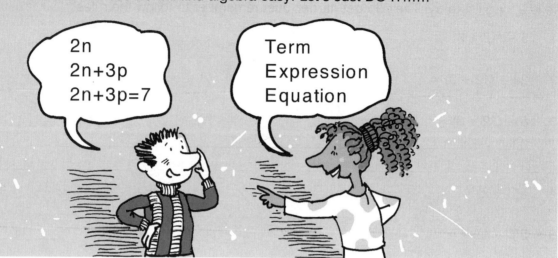

How to do it ...

Term

In **term**s of money, in **term**s of apples, in **term**s of anything ...

We use letters to represent different **unknowns** and each letter with or without a number in front is called a **term**.

So if n represents the cost of one plate then $4n$ means the cost of 4 plates, or 4 in terms of n.

$1p = p$

$3p$, $12p$, $2p$, p, $143p$ are all numbers in terms of p.

$4x$, $3y$, $12x$, $-6y$, $-13x$ are numbers in terms of x or y.

Expression

An **expression** consists of one or more **term**s and can also have numbers.
Each term is joined by an operation $(+, -, \times, \div)$.

e.g. $3p + 4q$ $12 + 3a$ $4n - 2n + 4$ $2x(4y - 3)^2$

Equation

When an expression is written as being equal to something then this is called an **equation**, as in the example:

$3x + 4 = 19$

It means: the expression $3x + 4$ is equal to the value 19.

8 Exercises

Now practise!

Write whether the following is a term, an expression or an equation.

1 $4k + 2 = 5$ _____

2 $345p$ _____

3 $23f^2 - 12$ _____

4 $4k + 2$ _____

5 $345p - 45$ _____

6 $23f^2 - 12 = 1$ _____

6

What are the unknowns used in the following expressions and equations?

7 $4n - 2n + 4$ _____

8 $4k + 2 = 5$ _____

9 $3p + 4q$ _____

3

8 Term, expression and equation continued

Writing expressions

Here are some examples of expressions.

Add 4 to a number.	$4 + n$	or	$x + 4$
Subtract 5 from a number.	$n - 5$	NOT	$5 - n$
Subtract a number from 9.	$9 - x$	NOT	$x - 9$

Multiply a number by 7. $7 \times n$ or $n \times 7$ but the simplest way of saying this is $7n$

Multiply a number by 4 then add 5. $4n + 5$

Multiply a number by itself. $p \times p$ but the simplest is p^2

Summary

Here are some examples of:

• **terms**	$3p$	$3a$	$-2n$	
• **expressions**	$3p$	$3p + 4q$	$12 + 3a$	$4n - 2n + 4$
• **equations**	$3p + 4q = 23$	$12 + 3a = 12$	$4n - 2n + 4 = 2$	

8 Exercises

Now practise!

Write an expression for these. Use n for the unknown number.

10 Add 7 to a number. _____

11 Subtract 4 from a number. _____

12 Multiply a number by 13. _____

13 Multiply a number by 6 then subtract 2. _____

14 Multiply a number by itself then add 3. _____

15 Add 5 to a number then multiply by 2 (be careful!). _____

6

9 Simplifying expressions

Brilliant idea. Let's make expressions simpler!

We can do this by collecting like terms (terms that are the same as each other) or removing brackets.

How to do it ...

Collecting like terms

$b + b + b = 3b$　　　　$n + n + n + n = 4n$　　　　$x + x + x - x = 2x$
$2b + 3b + 4b = 9b$　　$3n + n + 6n + n = 11n$　　$3x + x + x - 2x = 3x$

Collecting like terms in expressions with more than one term

$b + b + a = 2b + a$　　$n + p + n + p = 2n + 2p$　　$x + 3y + x - y = 2x + 2y$

Collecting like terms in expressions with number terms

$b + b + 6 = 2b + 6$　　$n + 8 + n + 8 = 2n + 16$　　$x + 3 + x - 1 = 2x + 2$

Multiplying over a bracket

$3(n + 4)$ is equal to $3n + 12$ because the 3 outside the brackets means 3 lots of everything in the brackets.

We can show this using the box method:

×	n	+4
3	$3n$	+12

$3(n + 4) = 3n + 12$

Summary

- $n + n + n + n = 4n$
- $n + p + n + p = 2n + 2p$
- $x + 3 + x - 1 = 2x + 2$
- $3(n + 4) = 3n + 12$

9 Exercises

Now practise!

Simplify the following expressions.

1 $c + c + c + c$ = _____

2 $c - c + 2c + c$ = _____

3 $3n + 4n + 6n + n$ = _____

3

4 $b + 3b + 6a$ = _____

5 $x + 3y + 5x - 2y$ = _____

6 $3n + 4p + 6p + n$ = _____

3

7 $b + 7 + 6b$ = _____

8 $h + 8 + h + 9$ = _____

9 $3n + 4p + 6p - n$ = _____

3

10 $2(b + 7)$ = _____

11 $5(h - 9)$ = _____

12 $3(6p + n)$ = _____

3

Simplify the following expressions. Remember the order of operations.

13 $b + 7 + 6(b + 4)$ = _____

14 $x + 3 + 5(x - 9)$ = _____

15 $3n - 4p + 2(6p + 1)$ = _____

3

10 Writing sequences from rules

We have seen sequences such as 5, 7, 9, 11, ... and we have described the rules.

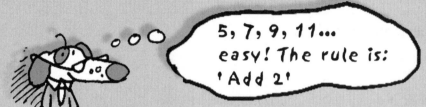

5, 7, 9, 11...
easy! The rule is:
'Add 2'

Now we will look at using some algebra and how to write the rules as expressions!!!

How to do it ...

Explaining the rule in words

We always need to know the first term and how we get from each term to the next.

e.g.   *5, 7, 9, 11, ...*

In this sequence the **first term** is 5 and the term-to-term **rule** is add 2.

Writing the rule as an expression for the nth term

We number the terms in the sequence 1, 2, 3 and so on, starting with the first term. We call this term number n.

e.g.   *5, 7, 9, 11, ... (1st term, 2nd term, 3rd term, 4th term, ...)*

Term number n	1	2	3	4	n
Term	5	7	9	11	—

+2

Where the term-to-term rule for the sequence is to add a number each time, we then multiply n by that number. In this example the rule is add 2, so we multiply n by 2.

Term number n	1	2	3	4	n	
Term	5	7	9	11	—	×2
Add 2 so $2n$ =	2	4	6	8	$2n$	

Now we work out what we need to do to $2n$ to get to each term.

Term number n	1	2	3	4	n	
Term	5	7	9	11	—	+3
Add 2 so $2n$ =	2	4	6	8	$2n$	
Add 3 to $2n$	2 + 3 = 5	4 + 3 = 7	6 + 3 = 9	8 + 3 = 11	$2n + 3$ = __	

So the expression for this sequence is $2n + 3$.

10 Exercises

Now practise!

Explain the following rules in words. Give the first term and the term-to-term rule.

1 4, 5, 6, 7, ... 1st term = _____   Rule = _____

2 13, 17, 21, 25, ... 1st term = _____   Rule = _____

3 20, 18, 16, 14, ... 1st term = _____   Rule = _____

4 15, 20, 25, 30, ... 1st term = _____   Rule = _____

5 7, 9, 11, 13, ... 1st term = _____   Rule = _____

6 30, 27, 24, 21, ... 1st term = _____   Rule = _____

12

Find the nth term of the following sequences using the tables to help you.

7 With the sequence 4, 5, 6, 7, ... The first term is _____ and the rule is _____

Term number n	1	2	3	4	n
Term	4	5	6	7	__
__ so __ n =	__	__	__	__	__n
Add __ to __ n	__ + __	__ + __	__ + __	__ + __	__n + __

The nth term is _____

8 With the sequence 13, 17, 21, 25, ...

Term number n	1	2	3	4	n
Term	__	__	__	__	__
__ so __ n =	__	__	__	__	__n
Add __ to __ n	__ + __	__ + __	__ + __	__ + __	__n + __

The nth term is _____

2

10 Writing sequences from rules continued

Finding the nth term in the sequence

To find term number n we work out $2n + 3$. e.g. *The 19th term is $2 \times 19 + 3 = 41$.*

Writing an expression for a decreasing sequence

We do this in just the same way as for an increasing sequence.

e.g. *22, 19, 16, 13 ...*

The **first term** is 22 and the term-to-term **rule** is $- 3$. Because the rule is take away 3 we multiply n by $- 3$.

Term number n	1	2	3	4	n
Term	22	19	16	13	__
Take away 3 so $-3n =$	$- 3$	$- 6$	$- 9$	$- 12$	$- 3n$
Add 25 to $-3n$	$- 3 + 25$ $= 22$	$- 6 + 25$ $= 19$	$- 9 + 25$ $= 16$	$- 12 + 25$ $= 13$	$- 3n + 25$ $=$ __

So the expression is $- 3n + 25$.
The nth term is $-3n + 25$. So the 50th term is $-3 \times 50 + 25 = -125$.

Summary

5, 7, 9, 11, ...

- The **first term** is 5 and the **rule** is add 2
- The nth term is $2n + 3$
- 1000th term is $2 \times 1000 + 3 = 2003$

22, 19, 16, 13, ...

- The nth term is $-3n + 25$

10 Exercises

Now practise!

9   15, 20, 25, 30, …   The nth term is _____

10 7, 9, 11, 13, …   The nth term is _____

2

The nth term of a sequence is given. Write the 10th term and the 100th term.

11 $n + 7$ 10th term = _____ 100th term = _____

12 $4n + 2$ 10th term = _____ 100th term = _____

13 $400 - 2n$ 10th term = _____ 100th term = _____

6

14   With the sequence 20, 18, 16, 14, …

Term number n	1	2	3	4	n
Term	__	__	__	__	__
__ so __n =	__	__	__	__	__n
Add __ to __n	__ + __	__ + __	__ + __	__ + __	__n + __

The nth term is _____

1

15   With the sequence 30, 27, 24, 21, …

Term number n	1	2	3	4	n
Term	__	__	__	__	__
__ so __n =	__	__	__	__	__n
Add __ to __n	__ + __	__ + __	__ + __	__ + __	__n + __

The nth term is _____

1

16   102, 96, 90, 84, …   The nth term is _____

1

11 Coordinate pairs on a line

(2, 3) is a coordinate pair and is also a point on a line!

So how do we put the two together?

How to do it ...

Coordinate pairs that follow a rule

(2, 3) is a coordinate pair. The 1st value is the x coordinate, the 2nd is the y coordinate. (x, y)

(2, **3**), (3, **4**), (7, **8**), (−2, **−1**) all satisfy the rule $y = x + 1$

In each coordinate pair, the y coordinate is one more than the x coordinate.

Using a table to find the coordinate pairs which satisfy a rule

The rule for a line is $y = 2x + 3$.

x	3	2	1	0	−1
$2x + 3$	2 × 3 + 3	2 × 2 + 3	2 × 1 + 3	2 × 0 + 3	2 × −1 + 3
y	9	7	5	3	1
(x, y)	(3, 9)	(2, 7)	(1, 5)	(0, 3)	(−1, 1)

The rule for a line is $y = 7 − 3x$.

x	3	2	1	0	−1
$7 − 3x$	7 − 3 × 3	7 − 3 × 2	7 − 3 × 1	7 − 3 × 0	7 − 3 × −1
y	−2	1	4	7	10
(x, y)	(3, −2)	(2, 1)	(1, 4)	(0, 7)	(−1, 10)

Summary

- (2, 3) is a coordinate pair. (x, y)
- (2, **3**) (3, **4**) (7, **8**) (−2, **−1**) are coordinate pairs and satisfy the rule $y = x + 1$
- Use a table to help you to find the coordinate pairs which satisfy a rule.

11 Exercises

Now practise!

Complete the coordinate tables below.

1 The rule for a line is $y = 2x + 5$

x	3	2	1	0	−1
$2x + 5$	2 × 3 + 5	2 × 2 + 5	2 × 1 + 5	2 × 0 + 5	2 ×−1 + 5
y	—	—	—	—	—
(x , y)	(__ , __)	(__ , __)	(__ , __)	(__ , __)	(__ , __)

5

2 The rule for a line is $y = 4x + 10$

x	3	2	1	0	−1
$4x + 10$	__ × 3 + __	__ × 2 + __	__ × 1 + __	__ × 0 + __	__ × −1 + __
y	—	—	—	—	—
(x , y)	(__ , __)	(__ ,)	(__ , __)	(__ , __)	(__ , __)

5

3 The rule for a line is $y = 7 - x$

x	3	2	1	0	−1
$7 - x$	7 − 1 × 3	7 − 1 ×__	7 − 1 ×__	7 − 1 ×__	7 − 1 ×__
y	—	—	—	—	—
(x , y)	(__ , __)	(__ , __)	(__ , __)	(__ , __)	(__ , __)

5

4 The rule for a line is $y = 4x + 1$

x	3	2	1	0	−1
(x , y)	(__ , __)	(__ , __)	(__ , __)	(__ , __)	(__ , __)

5

5 The rule for a line is $y = 16 - 2x$

x	3	2	1	0	−1
(x , y)	(__ , __)	(__ , __)	(__ , __)	(__ , __)	(__ , __)

5

6 The rule for a line is $y = 100 - 10x$

x	3	2	1	0	−1
(x , y)	(__ , __)	(__ , __)	(__ , __)	(__ , __)	(__ , __)

5

12 Using the correct notation in geometry

The more complex the geometry the more difficult it is to describe what we mean. So it is important to know the correct notation. We can use letters and symbols to help make things easier to understand.

How to do it ...

Line segments

A line segment is part of an infinite line. We label the ends of the line with capital letters.

e.g.

C ——————— D   G ———— H

Triangles

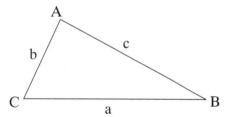

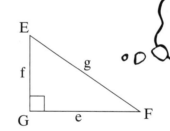

A right angle is marked with a small square at the vertex.

The vertices are written with capital letters and the sides are written with small case letters. The side written with small case c is opposite to Vertex C.

Parallel lines and lines of equal length

Parallel lines are marked with arrows on each line in the same direction. Lines of equal length are marked with identical dashes. For example, on this trapezium:

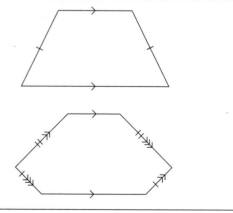

If there is more than one set of parallel lines then each pair have a different number of arrows. If there is more than one set of lines of equal length, then each set is marked with a different number of dashes.

Now practise!

Label the following line segments according to the following clues: the longest line is AB. The shortest line is GH. Remember to use capital letters.

1   Label the longest line AB.

2   Label the shortest line GH.

3   Label the remaining line ST.

3

Fill in the missing letters from these triangles, include all small case and capital letters.

4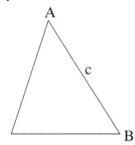

5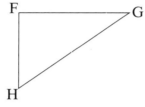

6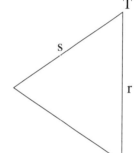

3

Mark all right angles, parallel lines and sides of equal length on the following shapes.

7

8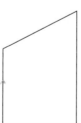

9

3

Angles

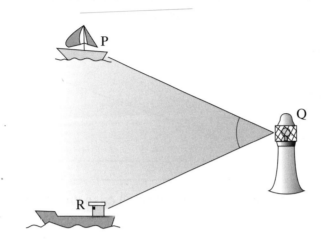

As the lighthouse at Q shines its beam of light, it turns. As it moves from shining it at the yacht at P to the boat at R, it turns through an angle.

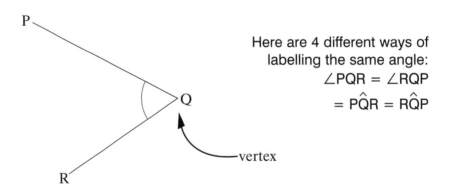

Here are 4 different ways of labelling the same angle:

$$\angle PQR = \angle RQP$$
$$= P\hat{Q}R = R\hat{Q}P$$

vertex

From now on we will label all verices with three capital letters, with the second letter being the vertex around which we are turning, e.g. $P\hat{Q}R$.

Summary

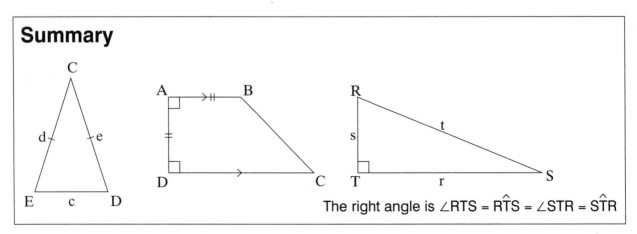

The right angle is $\angle RTS = R\hat{T}S = \angle STR = S\hat{T}R$

12 Exercises

Now practise!

Mark the following angles with a small arc.

e.g. ∠LMN

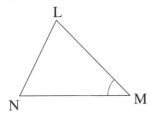

10 CD̂A

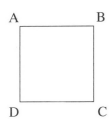

11 ∠HGF

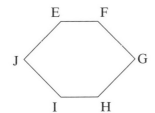

12 ∠KNM

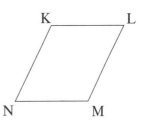

3

Name the marked angles on the diagrams below.

e.g.

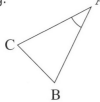

CÂB

13 _____

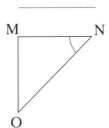

14 _____

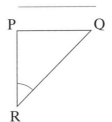

15 _____

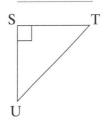

3

13 Angles on a straight line and vertically opposite angles

The sum of the angles at a point is 360°. If you remember this, these are easy!

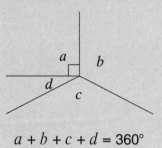

$$a + b + c + d = 360°$$

$$p + p + p = 180° = 3p$$
$$p = 60°$$

How to do it ...

Angles on a straight line

The sum of the angles on a straight line is 180°. This is because it is exactly half of the sum of the angles at a point.

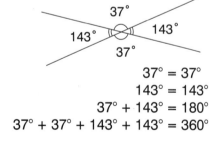

$$a + b + c = 180°$$

+

$$e + f + g + h = 180°$$

=

$$a + b + c + e + f + g + h = 360°$$

Vertically opposite angles

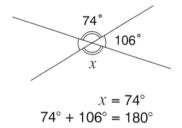

$$37° = 37°$$
$$143° = 143°$$
$$37° + 143° = 180°$$
$$37° + 37° + 143° + 143° = 360°$$

$$x = 74°$$
$$74° + 106° = 180°$$

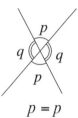

$$p = p$$
$$q = q$$
$$p + q = 180°$$

Any two lines **that are not parallel** intersect at a point if extended infinitely. They produce two pairs of vertically opposite angles where they intersect. **The opposite angles are equal.**

Summary

• Angles at a point add up to 360°.

• Vertically opposite angles are equal.

• Angles on a straight line add up to 180°.

13 Exercises

Now practise!

Find the value of the unknown angles.

1 $a =$ _____

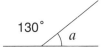

130° a

2 $b =$ _____

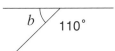

b 110°

3 $c =$ _____

45° c

4 $d =$ _____

d 102°

5 $e =$ _____

140°   40° e

6 $f =$ _____

157° f 23°   157°

6

Find the value of the unknown angles.

7 $g =$ _____

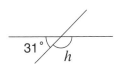

g 120°

8 $h =$ _____

31° h

9 $i =$ _____

i

10 $j =$ _____

54° j

11 $k =$ _____

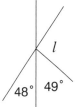

136° k

12 $l =$ _____

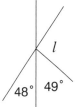

l 48°   49°

6

14 Rotation

We have seen rotation before so this will be easy!

All we will do is use the correct notation so that we all know what we are doing. And so we can tell other people!

How to do it ...

Notation

We always **rotate** an **object** about the **centre of rotation O** to the new position called the **image**.

If the direction is not given, the rotation is **anticlockwise**.

The vertices of the **object** are given by capital letters, such as **B**, **C**, **R**.

The vertices of the **image** are given with a dash that looks a bit like an apostrophe, such as **B′**, **C′**, **R′**.

e.g.   *Rotate the object* EFG *90°*
        about (1, 0) and draw its image.

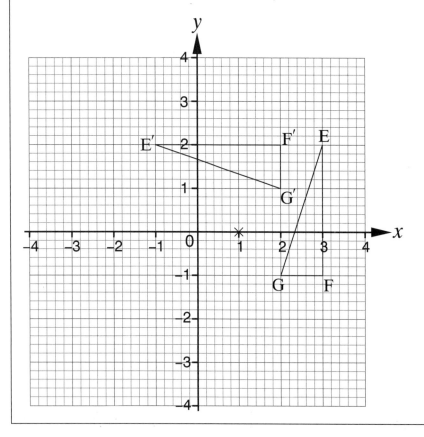

14 Exercises

Now practise!

Rotate the following shapes, labelling the vertices of the image on the diagram.

1 Rotate ABC about (0, 0) through 90˚.

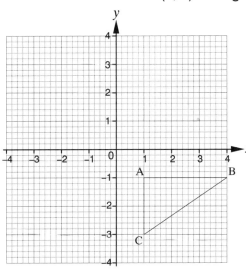

2 Rotate DEFG about (1, 0) through 180˚

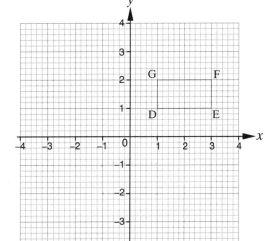

3 Rotate HIJ about (−1, −1) through 90˚ clockwise.

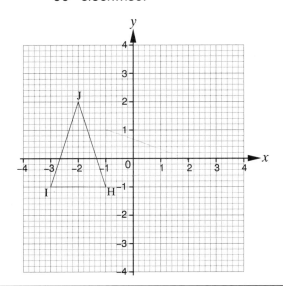

3

Rotational symmetry

A shape has **rotational symmetry** if it fits onto itself **more than once** during a complete turn.

The **order of rotational symmetry** is the number of times a shape fits onto itself during a complete turn.

e.g.

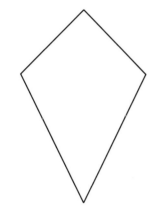

No rotational symmetry
(order 1)

(order 2)

(order 4)

Summary

- **Rotate the object round the centre of rotation O.**
- **If the direction is not given**, the rotation is **anticlockwise**.
- **object**   B, C, R,
- **image**   B′, C′, R′,
- The **order of rotational symmetry** is the number of times a shape fits onto itself during a complete turn.

Now practise!

Write the order of rotational symmetry of the following shapes.

4
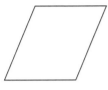

_____

5
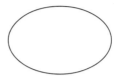

_____

6
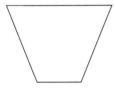

_____

7
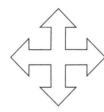

_____

8

_____

5

15 Surface area of cuboids

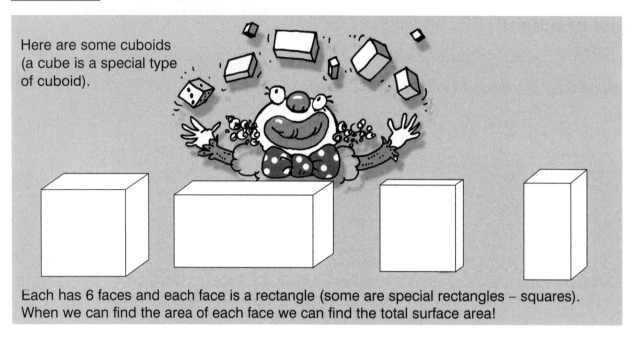

Here are some cuboids (a cube is a special type of cuboid).

Each has 6 faces and each face is a rectangle (some are special rectangles – squares). When we can find the area of each face we can find the total surface area!

How to do it ...

Finding the area of one face

5 cm | 7 cm

The area is 35 square centimetres written as 35 cm²

$Area = width \times height$
$= w \times h$
$= 7cm \times 5cm$
$= 35\ cm^2$

Surface area of a cuboid

A, B, C

h, l, w

5 cm, 7 cm, 4 cm

Surface area = 2A + 2B + 2C $= 2(7 \times 4) + 2(5 \times 7) + 2(5 \times 4) = 2lw + 2hl + 2hw$
$= 2(28) + 2(35) + 2(20)$
$= 56 + 70 + 40$
$= 166\ cm^2$

Summary

- Area $= width \times height$
  $= w \times h$

- 35 square centimetres is usually written as 35 cm²
- Surface area $= 2lw + 2hl + 2hw$

15 Exercises

Now practise!

Find the area of the following rectangles.

1

9 cm

11 cm

Area = _____ cm^2

2

5 m

13 m

Area = _____ m^2

3

2 km

4 km

Area = _____ km^2

3

Find the surface area of the following cuboids.

4

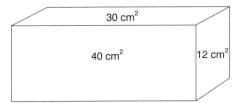

30 cm^2

40 cm^2

12 cm^2

Surface area = _____ cm^2

5

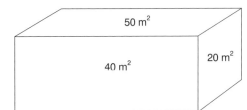

50 m^2

40 m^2

20 m^2

Surface area = _____ _____

6

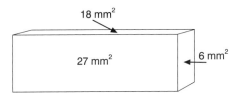

18 mm^2

27 mm^2

6 mm^2

Surface area = _____ _____

5

Find the surface area of the following cuboids.

7

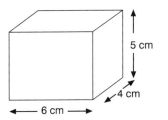

5 cm

4 cm

6 cm

Surface area = _____ cm^2

8

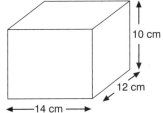

10 cm

12 cm

14 cm

Surface area = _____ _____

9

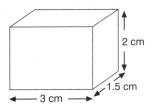

2 cm

1.5 cm

3 cm

Surface area = _____ _____

5

16 Range and median

You have probably been introduced to these words and know what they mean. If so, that's a great start!

But lots of mistakes are made with them, so let's make sure that you are not going to be the person who makes the mistake.

How to do it ...

Range

This is a number used to explain how wide the spread of data is.

It is found by taking the largest value away from the smallest value.

Range = **Maximum value** – *Minimum value*

e.g. Shoe sizes   3   8   4   5   2   9   11   4
      Range = **11 – 2 = 9**

The shoes are **spread across 9** different sizes. So we write that the range is 9, not 11 – 2!

Median of an odd number of terms

The median is the **middle** value **after ordering** all the values from smallest to largest.

e.g. Shoe sizes   3   8   4   5   2   9   4
      Ordered   2   3   4   4   5   8   9
      Median =   **4**

Median of an even number of terms

This is halfway between the middle two values. Add them together then divide by 2.

e.g. Shoe sizes   3   8   4   5   2   9   11   4
      Ordered   2   3   4   4   5   8   9   11
      Median = $\dfrac{4+5}{2}$ =   **4.5**

Summary

- Range = **Maximum value** – *Minimum value*
- Range is a **single value**
- The **median** is the middle value after ordering all the values from smallest to largest.
- The median of **an** even number of terms **is halfway between the middle two values**.

16 Exercises

Now practise!

Find the range of the following sets of values.

1	5	8	4	3	11	= _____
2	46	12	108	51		= _____
3	23	23	23			= _____
4	13	14	4	0	3	= _____
5	4	−2	0	−4	6	= _____
6	−7	−2	−14	−3		= _____

6

Find the median of the following sets of values.

7 5   8   4   3   11

_____ _____ _____ _____ _____   = _____

8 15   8   10

_____ _____ _____   = _____

9 5   8   4   3   11   0   3

_____ _____ _____ _____ _____ _____ _____   = _____

3

Find the median of the following sets of values.

10 5   8   4   3

_____ _____ _____ _____   = _____

11 15   8

_____ _____   = _____

12 5   8   4   3   11   0

_____ _____ _____ _____ _____ _____   = _____

3

17 Probability

Certain, unlikely, improbable, even chance, …

These are all a bit too vague.
Let's be a bit clearer about what we mean!

How to do it ...

Probability scale

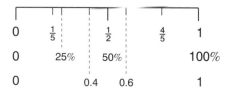

We can use fractions, decimals or percentages to describe probability.

You will probably start with fractions so that is what we will work on now.

Equally likely outcomes

If we roll a fair dice, we can get a 1, 2, 3, 4, 5 or 6.

These are called **outcomes**. They are all **equally likely** outcomes.

For equally likely outcomes the probability of an event $= \dfrac{\text{number of favourable outcomes}}{\text{number of possible outcomes}}$

So, the probability of getting a 5 or 6 with a fair dice $= \dfrac{2 \text{ favourable outcomes}}{6 \text{ possible outcomes}}$

$= \frac{2}{6}$ which is the same as $\frac{1}{3}$.

Summary

- All **probabilities lie between 0 and 1** and can be expressed as fractions, decimals or percentages

- Equally likely **outcomes** have an **equally likely** chance of happening

- The probability of an event $= \dfrac{\text{number of favourable outcomes}}{\text{number of possible outcomes}}$

17 Exercises

Now practise!

Finish the following lists of outcomes.

1 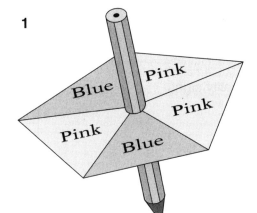   Blue, _____ , _____ , _____ , _____

2   Tossing a coin.   head, _____

3   Even numbers from 1 to 9 inclusive.   2, _____

4   Prime numbers on a dice.   _____

5   The letters in the word LUCK.   _____ , _____ , _____ , _____

6   Vowels in the alphabet   _____   **6**

Find the probabilities of the following.

7   Getting a 4 on a fair dice.   _____

8   Tossing a tail with a fair coin.   _____

9   Spinning Pink on the spinner in question 1.   _____

10   Picking a strawberry yoghurt from a pack of 2 raspberry, 2 black
    cherry and 2 strawberry.   _____   **4**

Test 1

Which number is bigger?

1   68.6   or   68.09   _____   **1**

Use the correct inequality sign (< or >) to show which number is bigger.

2   0.639   __   0.396   **1**

Place the following numbers on the correct sides of the inequality signs.

3   2.04   2.4   2.005   _____   <   _____   <   _____   **1**

Convert these measurements into the following units.

4   1.03 litre   = _____ cl   = _____ ml   **1**

Order these measurements, starting with the smallest.

5   21.3 cl   0.2 litre   203 ml   ____ ____ ____   **1**

Use the correct inequality sign to show which measurement is bigger.

6   41.5 cm   __   405 mm   **1**

Simplify the following.

7 $- -41$ _____

8 $-6 - 17 + -1$ _____

9 $-162 - +46$ _____   **3**

Find the answers to these.

10 $-5 + -4 =$ _____

11 $-407 - -13 + -2 =$ _____   **2**

Write whether the following is an expression or an equation.

12 $305p - 41 = 0$ _____

13 $3f^2 - 13$ _____   **2**

What are the unknowns used in the following expression?

14 $3p + 4q$ _____   **1**

Write an expression for these. Let the unknown number be n.

15 Add 201 to a number. _____

16 Multiply a number by 1004. _____

17 Multiply a number by 2 then subtract 1. _____   **3**

18 Using jK, label the following line segment correctly. (Be careful!)   **1**

_____

19 Write in the missing letters on triangle ABC. Include all lower case and capital letters.

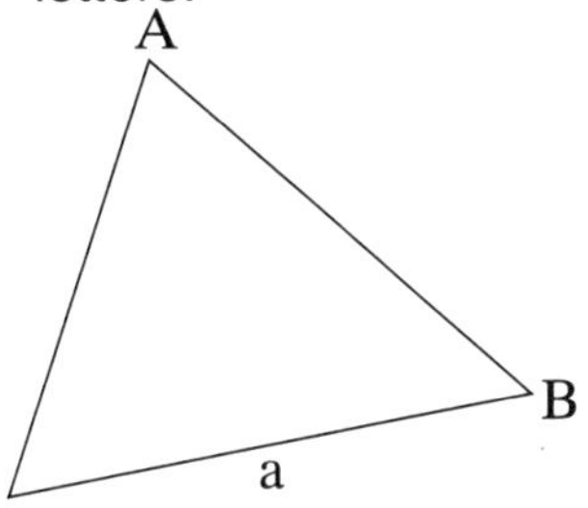

1

20 Mark all right angles, parallel lines and sides of equal length on the following shape.

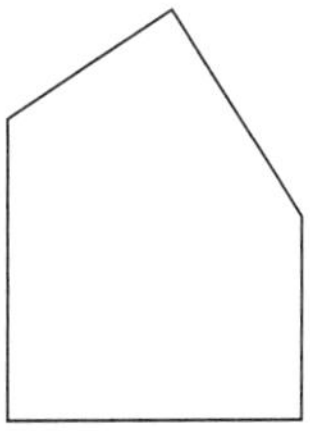

1

21 Mark the angle FGE with a small arc.

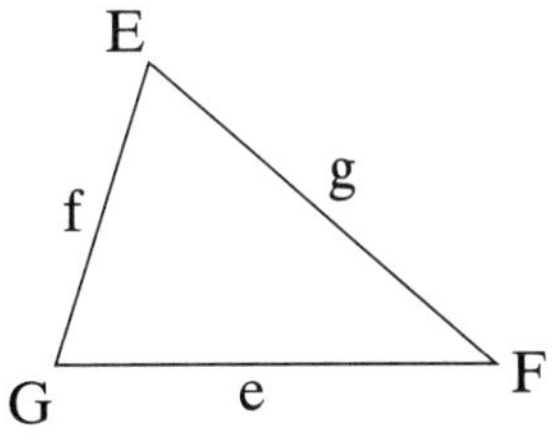

1

22 Name the marked angle on the diagram below.

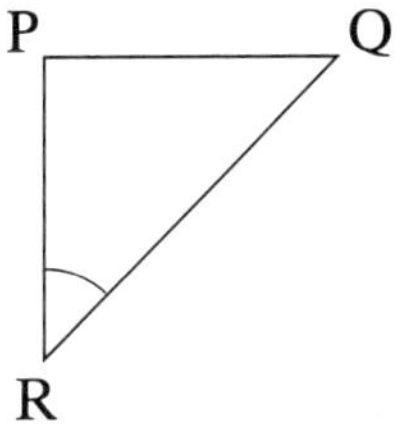

1

22 TOTAL

Test 2

1   What are the prime factors of 100?   _____   **1**

2   Write 48 as a product of prime factors.   48 = _____   **1**

3   Find the HCF of 56 and 42.   _____   **1**

4   Find the LCM of 18 and 10.   _____   **1**

Simplify the following expressions.

5    $c - c + 4c + 3c$ = _____

6    $x + 30y + 15x - 12y$ = _____

7    $12(h - 5)$ = _____

8    $5n - 2p + 3(3p + 6)$ = _____   **4**

9 Find the value of **a**.

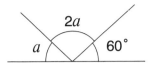

$a = $ _____   **1**

10 Find the value of **b**.

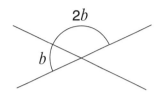

$b = $ _____   **1**

11 Find the range of the following set of values.

     −5   +8   4   13   −11   = _____   **1**

Find the median of the following sets of values.

12   15   18   14   13   21   10   13

   ___   ___   ___   ___   ___   ___   ___   = _____

13   105   108   104   103   111   100

   ___   ___   ___   ___   ___   ___   = _____   **2**

13
TOTAL

Test 3

1 Multiply the following number by itself to make a square number.

9 _____ | 1 |

2 $2 \times 2 = 2^2$. Write the following in the same way.

$19 \times 19 =$ _____ | 1 |

3 Find 11^2. _____ | 1 |

4 Find the square root of 64. _____ | 1 |

5 $\sqrt{81}$ = _____ | 1 |

6 $\sqrt{3600}$ = _____ | 1 |

7 $15 - (18 - 12)$ = _____ | 1 |

8 $5(4 - 2)$ = _____ | 1 |

9 $25 + 8^2$ = _____ | 1 |

10 $13 + 24 \div 3$ = _____ | 1 |

11 $6^2 + 2(25 \div 5) - 6$ = _____ | 1 |

12 Give the 1st term and the term-to-term rule of the following sequence.

15, 19, 23, 27, ...   1st term = _____   Rule = _____ | 2 |

13 The nth term of a sequence is given. Write the 8th term and the 80th term.

$3n + 2$ 8th term = _____   80th term = _____ | 2 |

14 For the sequence 51, 46, 41, 36, … complete the table to find the nth term.

Term Number n	1st	2nd	3rd	4th	n^{th}
Term	___	___	___	___	___
___ so ___ n	___ × 1st	___ × 2nd	___ × 3rd	___ × 4th	___
___ n	___	___	___	___	___ n
Add ___ to ___ n	___ + ___	___ + ___	___ + ___	___ + ___	___ n + ___

2

n^{th} term = _____

Rotate the following shape, labelling the vertices of the image on the diagram.

15 Rotate DEFG about (1, 0) through 90°.

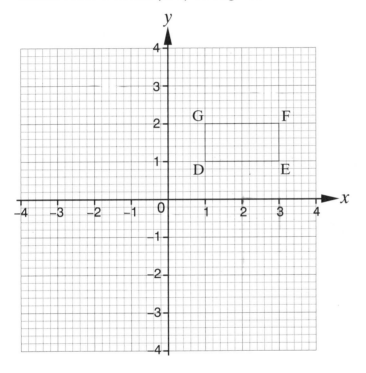

1

Give the order of rotational symmetry of the following shapes:

16

17

_____   _____

2

20
TOTAL

Test 4

Convert these fractions to hundredths.

1 $\frac{63}{10}$ _____

2 $\frac{66}{40}$ _____   **2**

Convert these fractions to decimals.

3 $\frac{7}{100}$ _____

4 $\frac{103}{100}$ _____

5 $\frac{3}{10}$ _____

6 $\frac{5}{20}$ _____

7 $\frac{28}{20}$ _____

8 $4\frac{9}{12}$ _____   **6**

Rewrite the following statements using the ratio symbol **:**

9   6 orange beads for every 11 blue beads.   _____

10   There is a 13 to 2 chance of winning.   _____   **2**

Put a line through the odd one out.

11   3 : 7   30 : 700   12 : 28   **1**

Fill in the missing number.

12   1 : 7   6 : _____

                    ×6   **1**

Share the following amount of money in the given ratio.

13   £80 in the ratio 3 : 1   _____   **1**

14 The rule for a line is $y = 3x - 4$. Complete the table.

x	3	2	1	0	−1
(x, y)	(___ , ___)	(___ , ___)	(___ , ___)	(___ , ___)	(___ , ___)

5

15 The rule for a line is $y = 5x + 2$. Complete the table.

x	3	2	1	0	−1
(x, y)	(___ , ___)	(___ , ___)	(___ , ___)	(___ , ___)	(___ , ___)

5

Find the area of the following rectangle.

16

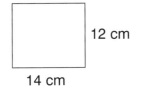

12 cm

14 cm

Area = _____ cm²   **1**

Find the surface area of the following cuboids.

17

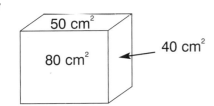

50 cm²

80 cm²

40 cm²

Surface area = _____ _____   **2**

18

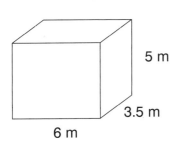

5 m

3.5 m

6 m

Surface area = _____ m²   **1**

Finish the following lists of outcomes.

19 Odd numbers from 10 to 18 inclusive.   11, _____

20 Non-prime numbers on a fair six-sided dice.   _____

2

Find the probabilities of the following.

21 Getting a 2 on a fair six-sided dice.   _____

22 Picking a red bead from a bag containing
3 green, 2 black and 4 red beads.   _____

2

31
TOTAL